THE SLEEP ORCHARD

(A Response to Arshile Gorky)

THE SLEEP ORCHARD

(A Response to Arshile Gorky)

Amy Dennis

Mansfield Press

Library and Archives Canada Cataloguing in Publication

Title: The sleep orchard : a response to the life and art of Arshile Gorky /
Amy Dennis.
Names: Dennis, Amy, author.
Description: Poems.
Identifiers: Canadiana 20220225729 | ISBN 9781771262804 (softcover)
Subjects: LCSH: Gorky, Arshile, 1904-1948—Poetry.
Classification: LCC PS8607.E56 S54 2022 | DDC C811/.6—dc23

Editor for the press: Stuart Ross
Cover design: Denis De Klerck
Cover art: Amy Dennis
Typesetting: Stuart Ross
Author photo: Victoria Dennis

The publication of *The Sleep Orchard* has been generously supported by
the Canada Council for the Arts and the Ontario Arts Council.

Mansfield Press Inc.
25 Mansfield Avenue, Toronto, Ontario, Canada M6J 2A9
Publisher: Denis De Klerck
www.mansfieldpress.net

CONTENTS

For my mother, Victoria Dennis.

For my lighthouse, Alberto Bassi.

ON WAKING

My lover says I have called out
while asleep for beetroot juice and saffron, declared
the colour of dove's blood is audible
and must

be written down. I don't remember.
But know after waking I've scavenged

old papers to find antique recipes for ink, hungry
for a hallowed liquid to write about Gorky. In dreams
he is tall and looks into me.

Every morning his paint rattles my thin grasp
on language.

GREENWARE

Colour, like every living thing, leaks
blood, but I've never before slit
my fingernails into this

wild apple and pistachio
where his mother wipes her hands. Her hemline,
in my mind, stitched damp

by me, kept moist in dark
corners—I can't stand
to let it dry. Colour, like anything

once alive, leaves scars. Red
ferric oxide and fire. Even my thumbs
dulled to a blind nub, because I've bitten, chipped

off the varnish. Naked, no pockets
for me to hide my hands. This, how
it is, spinning Arshile Gorky.

My clay fingers scorch
into brick, standing too close
to certain canvases.

ADMISSION

I know

I know
nothing

of Armenia 1915
pointed tip elliptical
from milk-

weeds
rupturing

is why I shut open
my eyes

outside
the door before
the punch

of the ticket
tell me

where to safe summer-
keep in me
sleep his sleep orchards

APPRENTICESHIP

In this first room, he starts
to sign artwork with his version
of a future

name. I read once
but don't remember
the string of sounds
his mother gave him at birth. I've never heard
in the flesh

his country's language. Downstairs,
the gift shop sells copies
of his letters: his penmanship
rhythmic, footprint

after footprint
from Anatolia, inking deep
into Syrian desert. His first attempts at forgetting
must have burned.

TATE MODERN, LONDON

These gallery rooms
housed boilers once. I still
feel the steam

leaking through as censor
saying I have no right
to liken a stranger's handwriting
to a death march. Some dropped
like full stops at the ends

of long sentences, low and un-
readable as ellipsis against the ground. In histories
like this, there are no—
What I mean is there are only
metaphors. Using image
as carapace, I stare

across the chasm, distance
between a spoken thing
and what

it really is. My own mother
still has the most beautiful hands;
it never pains me
to remember them.

THE ARTIST AND HIS MOTHER

Numb, colourless, his mother—
the forgotten curve of her
thumb against a blank

index finger. To feel again, he had to pierce
through all blisters, into the raw pink beneath
that he renamed
Arshile Gorky.
Every time he answered to this

in English, pins went in, and the serum
that spilled stayed with him. He used it
like turpentine to thin his paints, many
lost lives, and then his,
all dripping.

STAGNATION, SWELL,
A SUDDEN FLESHING

The artist,
his hands, his mother's absent
hands, painted over as clay blocks

because there's no real way
of reaching. At the ends
of our wrists: bricks. Are there fingers
beneath them? Taproot

deep in each of us, an image
instead of a name. Mauve violet—
less flower less petal less stem
than the inside of its scent

and tremor. Artist
in its quake, and the word *purple*, written
after an hour alone with his canvas, I can feel
nerve endings sprout through sidewalks
along the Thames. Someone said most poems
try to win back Eden. I was thinking this

in the Tate as the guard told me not
to stand so close; if only

I could have steadied
myself a half second from his paint
in the way I did close to the blue-
stones of Stonehenge. Armed with phosphor
and reverence for what's pregnant
and long dead, what truth

can there be in these hands
I've penned into earth-
enware pots? What blind warmth
in what embers inside them.

IN A SINGLE COCOON, A THOUSAND FEET OF SILK

Never buried
near Mont Sainte-Victoire: somehow, a shred
of Cezanne's cornea, Picasso's sinew
mistaken for thread. Ossicles, blunt
molar. A tailbone—sharp comma—that could have
belonged to either one. Gorky slept
with remnants of these two

artists under white
mulberry, ate only leaves, then spun
mosquito nets so we could see

clean into their billows, so small things
left of them could stay. Sometimes,

an insect

tried to inch in, but Gorky acted
on instinct before it could sting.

WOMAN WITH A PALETTE, 1927

More like a raw meat slab than a palette
in her lap—he never reworked this
canvas. Her eyes

have that uncooked look
of harbouring parasites, her stare
in the bloodstream for days. Dark rings

around eyes, echoing the black-
birds' incessant beaks that won't stop
the bringing.
Gorky hurled stones
at them from his studio window, then wept

the way one does when born, endless,
into the rust of closed doors that hurt
when pushed, pushed open

again. Tall, too heavy-knuckled,
he slumped under archways, empty-
echoing and clinging to random trivia
to make it through the day, fossil evidence
the rose predates humans—proof, sometimes, the delicate
survives—and in some religions, baptisms
for the dead: the living as the deceased
person's proxy. This woman, raw with palette,

is his mother, mother's sister, sister's daughter, anyone
he once knew with too little, all returned through him
in sacrament. Curved, at last, with comfort
into the canvas's hammock of Greco-Roman
folds—their faces, restful, rescued

from graves of yellow
rape fields into this calm. A Red Ochre
that lets the light through. Burnt Sienna, Terra Verde. Inside
his strokes, smoke mixes sugar and apricots leak
wasps. The fruit's stone,

opulent. Her eyes better
than a soul. To come yet, many more
charred beloveds.

FLAME AND SMOULDER

Gorky's hand inside the belly
of an iron stove, shifting logs that spark
scarlet, then roll

like burlesque hemlines
on 14th Street. New York, rapture
of claws and bruised calves in *The Liver
Is the Cock's Comb*, where oil caramelizes
canvas. Absinthe soaks flashbacks
locked with blue. The after-

taste a breakage of surfaces. Shallow pools
shatter with sparrows bathing; their wings
frenzied low fires

surging back, rabid,
in a corner against god, like his grandmother
setting the village altar ablaze—
first husband nailed dead to her
heavy church doors, first son a blood pulp
in the orchards.
And we feel alone

in the colours
with Gorky. Did he speak
seconds before he hanged
himself, or as he painted his eyes into oak
leaves? From them, could he feel the self-
portrait say *YES yes*

to his wife's unpunctuated skin, to the lit
pyre, birch twigs and linden. Nests
of tinder. Then the peace of nothing left to burn.

TRACKING DOWN GUILTLESS DOVES, **1936**

But toward the lower left, bent
at the elbow, black-tipped and cauterized
blue, there's a moss-covered crescent
I am hesitant to trust.
Its pthalo linked

with grit olive hues, brine-bitter
in eyes as wine vinegar. Hidden, the pigments
have formed trysts, fugitive
in jazz; think the Folies Bergère. Cinnabar
calves, colours between knees—viridian, sap cadmium pine,
peacock. If chartreuse was ever

used, it is now a cypress bruise, fern pupa, velvet
lime. Trying to place this tint
or gradation is like having to reiterate
what trees say across forests.

                           Hot rum, half drunk,
I don't know
what it is trees say across forests. From the city,
under neon, I sometimes see sometimes feel
them slow-dancing.

WOUNDED BIRDS, POVERTY,
AND ONE WHOLE WEEK OF RAIN

Gorky could see into the weeping
Guernica, their sky-
turned faces with jaws unhinged, an infant's
face vacant as though

floating in formaldehyde. Their core
ache the same as when he chased
cannonballs into crossfire
as a child, gauging what little
time left

to douse them. And like others
who survived by this sixth sense
in the war, it crept up on him
when least expected—

on a quiet bench in Central Park
with a friend, both witnessing a broken-
winged pigeon about to drown before
someone swam the pond to save it. When
the wet fury stilled

and the bird returned
to dry ground, Gorky broke
his breath to say
My God.

My God. I felt
the agony you had.

HIS WIFE, MOUGOUCH, AFTER HER AFFAIR WITH MATTA

I was unlit,
monochrome, not fattened with enough
wax when the wick inched its way out
of me for the surface, through organs,
breaking skin, naked,
inviting

fire. I burned, and my body
moved like a waterfall. Lush, electric-
surged, prismatic in how I answered

and sacrificed
my marriage. Moonstruck
raw, open for him

under the crystal liquids of a phosphor
chandelier—same light source,
years later, that the surrealists used,
blaming him for the suicide
of my husband, branding
his left breast with a hot iron, the word Sade
scorched over both

our breasts. Before
I took him as a lover, I knew
he could charm snakes—never
sewed any mouths shut for safety.
How can we, or rather, I [unfinished].

IN ARMENIA, PEOPLE TELL
THEIR BAD DREAMS
TO THE RUNNING WATER

In sleep, some still walk
the road to Yerevan, where crows battle
dogs for the dead. Eyes
of corpses closed to
become easier meat. Agonal
gasps, and dirt.
Horseshoes nailed bare
to feet. Folklore says
speak this

to the running water; the lucky
will lose

nightmares this way, into the whirlpool's
swallow. It stomachs shrapnel, massacres
in Lake Van, fields of cucumber turned black
with bodies. Has a vortex

strong enough to strip aphids
from trees, or soldiers'
filth from the skin of his mother.
                              He hovers
over the basin, watching
old nocturnes submerge then drain—
what stays

he reshapes
to the pelvic bone of a horse
he once compared to the *Winged
Victory*, to the membrane
of that calf's heart he cured

by hand, its flesh stretched
to an instrument he strums sometimes
in song.

CORNFIELD OF HEALTH, 1944

Between colours—
blank spaces like the whites of Gorky's
eyes. We see

into his seeing of us
as animals. In this cornfield,
we are animals with him. Canary-spread, he warm-
hovers us. I hold

my hand close to his canvas and feel a bit
of wing.

*

Gorky lifted

these colours up for us to float them, thinking
of his infant daughters, apricots he called
flirts of the sun. A part of him returned
into that small body of his silence

under the smoke-blackened dome
of a tiny stone church. He prayed
one day he would paint.

NIGHTTIME, ENIGMA, AND NOSTALGIA, C. 1931–32

Unlike the old masters, he is not bound
to the crucifix or the saints. Instead, de Chirico's
Fatal Temple becomes his nightlight on God, dense
hatchings of velvet black, bone etching. Eighty drawings

steeped in scratching, Salt's sovereign
flavour, without scent. Somewhere, Sisyphus,
tugged over

the pencilled fringe by Gorky's exquisite
pull, and since my gallery visit, as I dream,
the night slugs in my English garden
have doubled, restless,
lusting after fresh offerings
in the soil; every morning, their engravings
in the dirt around the dahlias—

And still, de Chirico, going deeper into Gorky's
bleeding, both probing what to love
if not the enigma. The sun sets, bending
every hook in the hallway
with the weight of growing
accustomed to this dark.

SHARDS

Under Cezanne's basket of apples, the draperies
look smashed. Someone asks *Is Gorky limited to imitation?*

His carbon hands press flat against other artists, then
fiddle their dimmer switches before he probes
his own

dark. I think I know, sonar, how he locates
shapes in these famous canyons:

> Matisse's *Red*
> *Studio*, Miro's *Still Life*
> *with Old Shoe*, Picasso's *Plaster*
> *Head*, *The City* by Léger.

Just as his paintings of jagged trees
smooth the expanse between leaves, he penetrates
where these artists end
and he began, began, his

beginning echoed in the whispering of
Vosdanig, Vartoosh, Shushan,
Vosdanig, Vartoosh, Shushan

> until their travelling names hit
> the limits of who he is
> and bounce

back to him as butter-
churns, flower mills, their rain-
windowing on gardens
bright in Sochi.

IMAGE IN KHORKOM

This painting makes me not care
that Ted Hughes never heard a nightingale.
Something else creeps in to fill
the void:

paint replaces a garden. We march
forward, like Gorky, threaded
with candlewicks. In certain lifetimes, spark

fire. Two-faced flames
illuminate and burn down
our birthplaces, empty rooms
in us mirrored with eyes

that are magpies. Mint crust of dirt
against grey, a lilac shade veined with something
Frankenstein. Inside, an embryo. Above, cinder-
shelled breasts foreshadow

de Kooning. Armed and wild-
flowering with a long blossomed
red tongue. Small hands.
Dark heart.

WHEN MY LOVER LOOKS
AT THE PAINTING AND ASKS,
I'M TOO TIRED TO DISCUSS
WITH MUCH DEPTH
TERRA COTTA, 1947

Obliging, in half sleep, I reach
for a small enclosed
zone of words that, bite-sized,
will slip down

his throat so he'll come
to know just enough

of how I see
the painting. *Split peach*, I say, *thin ochre drip,*
biomorphic, and am done with it. But he's a man asking
to be tied to the bed, a jasmine
needing trellis, so I tell him

> *raw lipped frazzled sawflies muscled waterfall winged suet.*

> *Starvation and crayon ventriloquism.* I say

> *flesh dead flower jellyfish, jalapeño.*

> *Centre carnival bud of mauve foxglove*

and he swallows. This, why
I love him as his stomach acid accepts
and digests. With abstract art,
the body eats. The mind
has nothing to do with it.

MEDITATION ON WHITE (TRACED BACKWARDS), RESPONSE TO *CHARRED BELOVED I*, 1946

Named after lilies, his mother Shushan warmed
her infants in cradles lined with sand, grew daughters
to face east and hail Mary. Each November, string-tied
from the ceilings, she dried pears, their skins distilled
with rippled sugar and the deathly

look of withdrawal, the fruits
parched as embalmed songbirds or small raptors
swathed in Egypt. Her one son, his voice-

box drowned with balsam, would not speak
until he was six, until six spoke only with birds. This,
a small sacrifice for the close studies of such wings, white
doves he let roost in his breaking.

FACE TO FACE
WITH HIS *AGONY*, 1947

Nerve endings
chatter darkly across
the bodies' blood
sky

and someone, as solace, offers
Whitman. I'm not thinking of grass
as the uncut hair of graves; there's nothing here
to suggest continuum.

No organs anymore
in Gorky's chest; only ragdolls
wound tight with black
twine. Red pigment limbs

hang low
toward

soaked corners. Battered,
stuffed with floss. Once, he could
keep afloat

for days, resting on white inside
milkweed. Now, the last

raven made raw.
Wax lustering.

UPON STEPPING AWAY
FROM *AGONY*, 1947

To remember perfectly
that pain, so he could sculpt it, Bernini
seared his own flesh against red
charcoal until his face in the screaming
mirror became flames
                    jaw line gashed—

under marble asp hair, carved marrow-
stab of the eyes' white fire. Agony

like this—the throbbed pitch of a dog's
whistle—one needs to be pierced
to comprehend it.

Those who can't
are blessed. Although

some want to know; I've seen them
crucify themselves at Easter in the Philippines—

their scream
like Bernini's.   But now, to stand near

                    Gorky's *Agony*, that oil on canvas
                    I can recognize clearly at certain times
                    in my life.

                    I need more
                    space between me

and those rib cage

                red hollows, those glowing
                petal-horrid
                orange torsos.

1940, NEW YORK, GORKY BEFRIENDS MONDRIAN

He liked the painterly.
He loved sensuality…
Flat things irritated him.
                              —Vaclav Vytlacil

Gorky rests his huge hand on the straight shoulder
        of Mondrian's suit, the pinstripes too thin
                to scaffold him or stop his raw slipping

                        into shapes so organic they swell
                seedpods. Thumb-split, tumid orbs held
        by pendulums on the diagonal. Thoughts
                like barn swallows, sky-vaulting.
                Semi-tones of wounded indigo.
                        As opposite,

Mondrian's calm mind steamrolls
between the untainted blamelessness
of flat red yellow blue, refining the barest bones
of equilibrium. Against the intricacy of trees,
he turns his back until branches blacken
into simple grids. Razor-straight

                        as Gorky, stretched in traction
        after the car crash, morphine no release. Doctors
                        hang weights to pull space
                        between vertebrae. Hospital walls
                so hot the white enamel weeps. Nurses try
        to realign his neck, but bone-deep, he knows

                        only to go forward
                by curving. Horizon, unlevel

37

as finger-rutted dough
    left to bake on clay
    walls, his days pull, marking
        earth like a hand-
            held plow.

ONE YEAR THE MILKWEED, 1944

In swamps, wet thickets
and shores, his brush
strokes grow four feet.
Only two
in sand and loam,
three in meadows
or along roadsides.
Up to six in savannas and abandoned fields.

Because yellow pigment mixed in linseed
oil is too heavy for wind to lift, insects
are responsible for cross-pollination;
they carry his cadmium and lemon ochre
in waxy masses on their back legs. Like Pollock
trapped in drink, most bottleneck flies die
trying, too anchored to carry this surreal
Eden. It's honey-

bees, strong-limbed, that deposit
between petals and pistil the thickened skins
of his opened paint, so ovaries know to swell
okra when approaching autumn. Framed
seed pods of his wisp filaments wait
to split. After everything, I want to give him
that weightlessness.

AESTHETICS, C. 1946.
(PENCIL AND COLOUR
CRAYON ON PAPER)

And the eyes, deep
as the nest of an empty bird. Out-
breath of Bluebeard. In-
breath, alive again, his wives. Wet
clouds in a colour sink, left soaking

by Kandinsky. Manuscripts, off centre
on a forest floor, their gilt
philosophy half compost half storm.

This, what exists
in his blurred greens and centre lemon, small lava
scorching agate under lace. That clipped corner
blue of my mother's eyes. Where

pilgrims crawled
on their knees.

IN THE WEEKS BEFORE GORKY'S DEATH, HE DISRUPTS HIS WIFE AS SHE READS TO HIM BY THE FIRE

Days, like fingers, twist
their battalions
—Paul Éluard

Negative
space is what shapes us, he says, starting to un-
hear her. Revenants, one and all, we

are pitiful, afraid, ragged
as colour's edge on a Rothko.

LAST SKINS

No lilacs left as ransom
for the crossing of River Styx.

The dull dawn talks of lobotomy.
Black dog, done wrestling. Silence

between his wife's words
swells to the other side
of the glass, where flying snow
owls are the snuffing out
of a white candle.

TO PROJECT, TO CONJURE, 1944

How to say the word
for that rug-burned streak of flood-

water without blessing
where your children were left

to smudge their hands? Although I know
it sounds warm

to the skin, like amber,
and will not float

in brine. It stings, smells
of clean sweat and brown sugar, unlike

lapis or impasto jade. Pollock
said it should risk more

ugliness, and ugliness has its small part
in what I strive to pull

through my trachea like a bloodless
apple gall. How to mouth

a clenched blossom
shut by wasps? If only

I could say
in one syllable

or two why swifts
don't touch the ground

the first three years
of their lives.

I'M LOOKING AT YOUR *LOVE OF THE NEW GUN*, REALIZING

you'd never seen
real fireflies or milkweeds
prior to Virginia, though

already they lived
alongside your red
blood cells'

minuscule
cinnamon hearts, and taste-
buds, tiny land

mines that tore
insects and plants
apart. You painted

their shrapnel until antennas
embedded themselves in silk
floss and white

milk—into your quiet
but sometimes violent bio-
luminescence—its veiled

drip

a dull glow, quartz-
clouded. Because nothing
travels faster without mercy

than light, I will never turn
from your metal grasslands
of living

triggers. Long known, these are old
points of entry in us both, swollen
before we were born.

ONE THING SHIFTS
INTO ANOTHER, GORKY
DANCES WITH KNIVES

Withdrawal into woodwind and cymbal, he begins
slapping his thighs with the blades. Squat low, blood opus. Slipping
on a scratched floor, on tracked clay

and wet confetti where his nicked skin leaks the future
of de Kooning's Pink Angels. Fated, there'll be something of Gorky's
past
in their snow flesh and shut eyes. *Why*

is back the most beautiful direction? I can't lie
and say I see wings there. Only henna, the pale tenderness found
under a scab. When de Kooning returns

to retrace Gorky's dance moves with charcoal, he'll fill
the scuffed shapes with candy floss and mandarin, needing
to sweeten lines that sway like black ropes.

FROM THE MOMENT
A MAN IS BORN, HE LOOKS
FOR A PEACEFUL CRADLE

The same way heat rises
in a kitchen slowly filling with bodies, I'm starting
to understand—you turned,
imaginary, the smoking metal
against yourself

and the pooled lilacs coalesced, slanting
in conflicted waters. This, what one calls
Breton's impeccable arrow of light. You picnicked
the dunes in that light, swam Cape Cod naked, drew
elaborate pictures with hydrangea sticks
in wet sand. Rose

to your full height in the twilight
to emit a cry, tender and loud, like shepherds
of your native land. Anyone watching
would have said

you had a thousand years left,
that square of your shoulders
so timeless, the muddied pigment
under your fingernails
impossible
to imagine not there.

MOUGOUCH

Under her glass skin, close
to the surface, he leaves shredded violets
and vanquished berries. She stares
at them, unsure how to surrender.
The best thing

one can do when it's raining,
she learned reading Longfellow,
is to let it rain, so she reaches for a paint brush
still wet from being cleaned, uses it
to skim

the bruises, burnish
them with thin watered gloss
into a Triumph
of Bacchus. She arches
her back, breastbone flat
against a blood-grape sky. Her navel
the backdrop

to a crown of vines. Inspired by Velázquez,
she is too young to know so much light
on a man's flesh will make him look sick,
or that her crushed body, if she stays,
will remain only velvet
for a tired satyr.

APOLOGY FOR SHREDDED VIOLETS, VANQUISHED BERRIES

They sound beautiful—crushed blue, acai quelled. Crown
chakra the colour of good judgment. Tri-coloured violas
sugared for guests, glinting on royal icing. I lost

control, became sick, didn't stop
filtering your skin with diminutive
flowers, soaking your red
currents in sloe gin; instead

of violence, I wrote *violets*.

MARNY GEORGE
AT 36 UNION SQUARE

For six weeks, I didn't leave
your studio, sat on covered horsehair
wearing your grandmother's jewels—papier-mâché
weightless on my wrists and earlobes. Dark

in our sockets, insects droned, and I believed
you'd be a prophet. Tiny mites
reddened your eyes. We were poor,
no doctor to heal us. I don't know

who paid our rent; people say there were other
women, liquid with sugared gin
when you sat next to them and told them
your stories. You were a Russian portraitist,

Georgian prince, nephew to Maxim Gorky. Prodigy
who once studied in Paris. I, like them, assumed
it was all true, allowed your layers of vegetables and moon-
shine on our table. *An edible still life*, you said then,

for the bride: black earth on my fingers
after scraping carrots clean, then leaning
them against cabbages, aubergines until
their ochre flamed along jade

and I touched you. As you painted, I touched
to get close. You brushed through watered blood
of cut beefsteak—still fresh with scent
off the vine. Tender, onto the canvas

those nights, tender to my cool bare thigh.

*

I would like to be Mrs. Gorky, I wrote
on the crust

of a breadstick at Ticino's, then said yes
on the Brooklyn Bridge.

You bloodied my mouth:
our marriage

birthmark, broke my teeth
on your butter-churned mind.

In crumbs and cracked
sidewalks we found

orchids and fur, naked
under your poems

and my small gardenia.
Abstract, our days then.

We lived instantly
as acts of recognition.

*

Smoking, I watched you, over-
ripe with abandonment in 36 Union Square,
while other artists talked Rothko on 23rd Street,
of his *Sculptress*, said the only way out

is inward, while you strived to show all
sides at once, and in each
a new door, your palette morphed
cornflowers into flotsam into your mother's

threadbare dress. Dense pigments her oil-damp
hair, fastened with ink-hatched shells. You said
she smelled of storm-ocean. And I, a hue of orange.

*

You loved me because I looked
like that period of Picasso
when the walls were taken off
Pompeii. My pelvic cradle

a lava pond
filled with pottery
and ancient shards. I am almost dead
now. And you are ash in the meadow.

On our old street
in New York, 1934 scratches
like a dark beetle trapped
in a steel drain; there were
hallways behind
your sad eyes.

Living with you
was the closest I've come
to prayer.

*

After me, you'll find another wife
who'll lay out her white body

like a sepulchre. When it suits
you, you'll crawl

inside until she rises
and leaves. You'll be

a bag of stones. I close
myself against her

long limbs, let them
contour what

your life was.
Right now,

she's listening, shifting
like a Calder mobile in the yard.

*

Everything I write to you
is a woven prelude to small flight,
and in your paintings, peacocks lift
to the limits of trees. Husband, your beauty's
heaviness does not know

sky. I've seen you in books
still unwritten, in rivers where nothing
floats. I got close enough to touch

your barriers, your broken
ink on the tablecloths of our old haunts.

LATE FEBRUARY

Year before last, late February, the man I didn't know
I would marry caught a peacock moth in his car
and carried it to me with tranquil fingers. Those days,

I first laid myself bare to Gorky, beginning
with his mother's hands. I wanted to uncover

them, put blossoms on her
stump wrists at the end of which are bricks. I wanted
to lift every brick to build walls, where, safe
behind them, she could release something winged
from her palm and, with new hands, hold close to Gorky.

But to lift the bricks from his paintings would be to rip
his skin, his mother's skin, so I stepped a distance
back, started to feel my way through

his fields of grass scattered with snakeroot.

I READ ASH LIKE TEA LEAVES, TELL MYSELF I WOULD HAVE PLAYED A ROLE IN HIS BREAKING

Unlike you, Mougouch, I wouldn't have found
the volcanic stones, nor sewn amulets
for so long under his hemlines. His amber, in my house,
would have grown cold—never crushed with honey
as a cure. I would have let him sit alone

on strangers' doorsteps, stroking
our daughters' ragdolls. And if he'd been my lover
in Ancient Egypt, I wouldn't have embalmed
his heart, unable to touch so much
death and colour.

AMBIGUOUS SPACE, SEEMINGLY RANDOM ANGLES

Beneath this canvas is the seventeenth century, where
debts are paid with rose water.

*Pollock and Rothko and Gottlieb and de Kooning found themselves
after the death of Gorky.* In France, young girls were warned
not to smell the tuberose after dark.

When Mougouch spoke his real name more than a decade
after his death, her mouth spilled finches shaped with soot.

Shapes shut me out and draw me in like the river did
when I was a child, ringing knees against a crisp bell hem,
floating apples, like him, along the current.

There are paintings that make birds slip through
my skeleton. Fissionable, precise, petrol blue.

Nettles that grow over buried bodies reach a foot higher
than they would elsewhere. Eyebright, too white, my love
for trilliums.

Brush strokes stretch as far as my mother's
perfume when everything I wore she had sewn. Back then,
her hands appliquéd until the days ate us.

Pure, almost vacant, some textures one must enter
to make them talk.

TRIPTYCH FOR MOUGOUCH

[…] our life, the small part that I may have been in his life all
considered, that it was what it seemed to be, it was love and painting
and roses and thorns and dark and light, all the things that got lost
in a survey of facts and analysis.
—Mougouch, in a letter to Ethel Schwabacher

You always knew
that beside you, at night, he nightmared
the apricot trees, turned twigs into whips
and tempted fate. Air through his lungs
disturbed the Dead Sea but when you looked
in his palms you saw only fledglings.
I can't ever know

because a lake this dark has no mouth
and a mystery like his
aches when it is almost
recognized.

                            *

Loose ends will always swim
in you, Mougouch, your body locked
in his living embroidery, once stitched
as a foliage cry. Your thoughts

thicken over his
opened paints as cataracts
over eyes, or scales scraped
from Betta splendens.

*

I've heard people who go blind
can sometimes see in their dreams.
What is it you see in his dreams, these decades
after his death?

It cannot be helped—the eye closes
shapes to complete the circle.

DEAR ONE ABSENT
THIS LONG WHILE

I can't say I've ever seen
a ghost, or would believe it
if one looked back at me
over its translucent shoulder
before slipping

into another glaze, but perhaps
there was something of you
under our Victoria plum when the branches
were treble-bare or when I woke
this morning to find crocuses
blood-let by last night's frost.
This winter

there has been so much
effort, Egyptian onions still abound
under the freeze, and the redwings, flown
from Iceland, have willed
the birdbath to thaw. I've thought,
more than once, that you too
could have come through

to this other side, now
time has passed and the black carbon
of charred bones no longer shadows you
for its flesh, your old suicide shed
in the soft jaws of white
camellia; their petals
are your semi-tones,
your layered silence.

STUDIO FIRE, 1946

I think our lives flow like a molten lava.
—Arshile Gorky

A fire like Golgotha, according to your wife, *but as calamities go*
it had its exhilarating sides, persimmon charred red to mulberry, fast-
forwarded on a time-lapsed camera. You swam

in surrealist fashion, sky-miner, while those around you quoted
Thoreau. This was two years before your death, just after
the embers quelled. *I am convinced that I cannot exaggerate enough*
to even lay the foundation.

*

A smoke sky with crane flies
as salvaged fractions of your own
mind. Panic

hands cupped
bric-à-brac —less than a minute's
fistful. Cinders

that were your easel
blew cool
across grass.

*

Like common water pepper, your psyche
had already rooted where it was too flooded to burn,
and like its stem, your strength did not snap
into realgar—that dirt ruby made from arsenic
that burns with a blue flame.

62

*

You didn't forget
your mother's photograph
in the flames, her face
under soot like Earl Grey that has lined
the stomach. And your paintings
of her remain almost
angora: no dry academic dust, nothing cold
as Lucretia sleeping

since your studio burned
to the ground. On the ground,
on your knees, Kandinsky began to blur
with Hopkins' dragonflies

drawing flame until you opened
and spoke her name, quiet as clover.
It strengthened you.

THIS POEM CANNOT BE TITLED

You fed on what absence there is
in abstraction, its inability to pin
things down. While you under-

scored alphabets with feathered onions, others closed
your canvas as a coffin. They wouldn't have known
that this close to the edge, there's nothing

more alive than survival, yours heightened
by brocade and Baudelaire—the complexities
of your fauna confronting loss. Your mother,
not here

in field chicory or phlox. Your sisters, not
in the orange hawkweed. At the end of your life,
you never aligned with the recognizable—still hiding
what you loved from the Turks.

ANDRÉ BRETON HELPS
GORKY TITLE HIS WORK

Something dark strawberry, intense.
Then Breton, through the same membrane:

> *The Leaf of the Artichoke Is an Owl*
> *Water of the Flowery Mill*
> *How My Mother's Embroidered Apron Unfolds in My Life*
> *Love of a New Gun*
> *The Dervish in the Tree*

And they continue. Breton's heart
a shallow bowl, Gorky's
a cascade of berries.

RESPONSE TO SHADES OF YELLOW
IN THE *BETROTHAL II*, 1947

It feels like something close
to Fra Angelico's halos, although
oxide and tin lead are too metallic, and egg tempera
too much of a gloss. The truth must lie
somewhere in the small clash

between lemon   and cadmium,
cobalt or chrome   and ochre,
                       where these colours
                       share a room with two names
                       for one man: the differences
                       unspeakable.

WINDOWSILLS

Gorky's yellowed tips, still
in my neighbour's sun-
flowers despite this August
of drought, the crisp petals
pinched thin. They are too brittle
to touch, so I try
to speak them.

GORKY FINDS A PHOTOGRAPH
OF HIS MOTHER, FORGOTTEN
IN HIS FATHER SEDRAK'S DRAWER

Did Sedrak feel pulled by the portrait he left
in his drawer: her face—unframed,
scratched under a scattering.

She starved. He slept
every night, clothed, with a hatchet. Who knows

what his death meant for Gorky, whether it swelled
the expanse of whale ribs or Faust, if it echoed in him
as folklore. Or, like the quick sting of sulfur
against phosphorus, the pain was small—the first strike
of a match when one leans in too close
to the flare.

GRIEF HAS NO WORDS, ONLY A TRAILING OFF INTO THINGS REMEMBERED INACCURATELY (*MAKING THE CALENDAR*), 1947

This grey was once
made from the soot
of oil lamps. In its light, there were
voices. Small flecks, almost

unseen, the shredded fourth luck
of a clover. I once found
a lucky clover, or a lover found it
for me when my throat was beginning

to open. Open, it was
white, like the spaces in this
canvas, its lost hours. Under
lamplight, yes, there used to be

voices, someone's needle
from a record player etching
into paint and soaring en route
to me, unsteady, the dark June
bugs of Gorky's tremor.

HALF CITADEL, HALF CRÈCHE

From the smouldering, you made yourself
a half citadel, half crèche, where you rested with
hands seared in embers, for a while you stayed alive
like an insect living in fire-softened wood.

In a half citadel, half crèche, you rested with
sick pigments under the skin, cancer in your colon
like an insect living in fire-softened wood.
The wound in your side, leaking waste. Seeping

sick. Pigments under the skin, cancer. On your colon,
a stinging anemone, a spider enemy weeping
through the wound in your side, leaking waste. Seeping
through words and paint that couldn't save you from

that stinging anemone, that spider enemy, weeping
that bled you raw as Rembrandt's ox carcass, splayed
words and paint that could have saved you from
what waited: soldiers of hemlock, incessant nettle

that bled you raw as Rembrandt's ox carcass, splayed
hands. Seared in embers for a while, you stayed. Alive,
waiting for the soldiers of hemlock, the incessant nettle.
From these smoulderings, you made yourself.

WITHOUT REST

There is a kind of pressure in humans to take
whatever is most loved by them
and smash it.
—Anne Carson, "Book of Isaiah"

Your foot
steady on the plank, you razed
into a splintered wreck
and bruised

your wife, Mougouch, threw her
down the stairs when you thought she broke you.
In your earlier work the weight of that
violence is laid thick, surfaces textured, trying
to heal like a scab, the same grit and closeness
to cracking. On your canvases,
when the fluid beneath started

speaking, your edges
dissolved in threads. They dripped
to my lap. I look

down. Don't know how
to hold your heat your tenderness your good
hope roads, pastorals, your plow songs, how to link them
with you raising your hand against a woman.

UNQUIET

If anything blooms, it blooms

without a heart. How to describe

his life to a stranger

asking? That he came from a place

where apricots and walnuts were bartered

for cloth, and that already in the blue

void of his dreams, Miró's seedlings

were spiders crossing

dead men's torsos. Shapelessness

starvation's mother—has come through

in him

to the other side, where dried rib cages

sprout.

MUSCLES AND TENDONS,
CONTINUED LINES

*[T]he truth was that he had a deep visceral passion for making lines
flow from his hand onto paper. He amazed friends by whipping out a
Rembrandt or a Matisse on a cafeteria napkin.*
—Hayden Herrera

Remembering Rembrandt's *Anatomy Lesson of Dr. Nicolaes Tulp*, how
muscles and tendons of the lower arm are interrupted by a cold
instrument, I want to hold that instrument until it's warm, and as
conduit, continue the lines like Gorky on a cafeteria napkin, flowing
as though Matisse is standing behind, beginning to say something
of what's really going on in an alphabet where echoes are patterns
of Islamic art and everyone has enough guts not to fill things in
because, as Mallarmé says, this is a *Virgin, vivacious, / beautifully present day*
and my inside mind reminds of Matisse's *Red Studio*, no shadows but a
glint of sun where he drank wine, and I want to survey myself like
Rembrandt, without vanity although now there's a baby inside and
I can't bring myself to think of his dead children so I channel Gorky
scrubbing his floor, beads of splattered bleach on the vase collection
he liked heavy with dust—without fear how it filters the light, unquiet.

DEAR NATASHA (RESPONSE TO GORKY'S YOUNGEST DAUGHTER)

A kind of water, a kind of weight that will never
rise. I want to grasp the ends, the endings. Keep tripping
on skipping ropes, those turned and left
too fast, kids called in early from concrete. I hear
their hunger as a kind of buzz, the younger ones
with wings two hundred beats per second, speeding
and blind, their fast beauty like honeybees—
their brains the size of sesame seeds, yet their
calculations more complex
than criticisms I've seen of Rilke, who's been
called sentimental, refusing on his death-
bed a priest, believing instead
in the likeness of rose petals to eyelids, in tiny webs
that pull us taut, then slacken. Natasha, he called you
his little pine tree. Two days before
you were born, the bomb fell
on Hiroshima and I hate
that saying, *We learn little
from victory, much from defeat,*
because if your father wasn't dead, we could
go back, past rot, to root more
time in his hands.

FOR MARO, GORKY'S FIRST-BORN, WHO WAS SENT TO BOARDING SCHOOL WITH HER SISTER SHORTLY AFTER HIS DEATH

Like staring at flake white
for too long,

little girls can be cruel.
Thorns and antlers aimed
at you, eldest spawn of a dead artist
from Armenia. Small sister—still
wetting the bed.

Where to begin
with two children
who last lived with glass windows
for walls?

Don't choke
on iced honey from your parents' throats, their sallow lacquer
instead of snow. Don't survive as cold flesh locked

      in resin.

               I've seen a hummingbird egg, glaciate
               in frozen amber, also feathers and webs.
               A stamen with a scattering of pollen
               in the cinch of a frigid gold.

This arctic reverse of sun stole your father, his voice
apricot gone vinegar. I too have had to learn
that heating amber makes it soften.

(IN THE VOICE OF NATASHA)
THEY HAVE TAKEN MY ISLAND

And all I have left
are these stairs. The steps
sparse, feeling curved as a lurch
in the stomach.
      My sister
Maro says she remembers—
         dragging
         me waking
         us up the gradations
         until we saw

         our father naked
         as a glass tower
         without reflection.
         And below him,
         our mother, cowering.

Step

                     forward, step

back.

         There's been no rest.
         I reach

like Miro's dream
ladder until my radius and ulna
twist a painted black strand
with no body on either side, nothing
to float on water, no plateaus
where I can ask ghosts

to solder my thinnest lines, enclose
in archipelagos this shrapnel.

My sister Maro says
she remembers, but

> *shhhhhhhhhhhhhh*
> *shhhhhhhhhhhhhh*

> something cries
> when I try the landing.

THINGS DISSOLVE
IN PAINT THINNER THE WAY THE BEATEN DO
WITH DRINK

My liver
is sick
with purple

for this sparrow
artist, bursting. Gorky's milkweed

deities and beech leaves, raw
as Chaim Soutine, who thrust

                butcher's blood over
                    bled meat
        to bring the ochre back

                from the first red.
These tertiaries—something small
slaughtered in me when I see them

so I seek amity
from primary colours—can trust
they haven't touched anything
hidden that could hurt.

TULIPS, DE KOONING'S DAUGHTER, AND COPPER

Maro, there are two cut tulips in the foreground
of that photograph, the one where you overlap
Lisa, de Kooning's daughter. With thin wrists
slanting in, she is blond, elbows bent
around your neck, echoing

her father's earliest days
on Union Square when, slender, he angled in
to the scaffold of your father. Here
you are the stem that touches the bottom
of the vase in the centre and your jaw
is strong. Your face, open and unafraid
like the petal's parrot flame

and there's an old wives' tale
that if a copper penny is dropped
in a tulip's water, it won't wilt. You don't
wilt. There's a spur of light behind
that already speaks—if there is copper
in your water, it's a conduit, could ward off
cholera or cure open wounds, eat algae
until the glass where you live is clear.

Cut from the bulb, you grow
on your own. I could never
write your voice through first person.

AFTER HIS DEATH

Phantoms fed us chalk, then starved us of sugar.
We said they shouldn't flay
a dead dog.

Those of us who loved him were wrapped
in a numb hush. Snakes laid low
in the grass.

No more Coptic embroideries, better than Matisse.
No more scattered candles around holy trees, a long-dead pine in
    Armenia.
No more eggs simmered with onion skins so shells turned reddish
    brown.
No more orphan eyes, cut like the cry of a shepherd.
No more red cardinals that have not caught reflection.
No more friends like the Marquis de Sade.

Days passed

like a spider's egg sac
becoming swollen. Soon,

de Kooning, shattered, became his own
sentry, entering dark attics to excavate.

The soft edges of Rothko floated through a large rectangle mouth.

Rauschenberg was silent, cemented by what he erased.

Motherwell, from the gut, beside chloride that glittered
nickel, crystal, a basket and a boy of lime.

Coal black, Franz Kline, the hurting kind of light in white layers.

And at the top—King Pollock. Gothic. Alcoholic. Apex
of the avant-garde. He picked up his canvas. He
put it on the floor.

NINE MONTHS

Nine months pregnant, I can now
begin to reach what it must have been
for you to live and paint with children. From under my rib
as I write you, a tiny foot tries to press through
in the shape

of your biomorphics—rounded, smooth, as surreal
and inside as your moving contour—and all I can think of
are your shifts of raw pigment against this one body
of mine, stretching out, soon, into two. And then,
the splitting off again. April 1943, I dreamt

      your wife's amniotic fluids pool
      the cinema floor, morph concentric red
      under the exit sign. Something unpainted
      begins to cascade and when they ask
      for the baby's name, you say

      Maro. In your bones—
      her new blood, this small bringer of sky, a milk-
      pod daughter from long grasses
      and crayons waxed

      between fingers and thumb, all of her
      itching to be tree-limbed and lichen. Her irises
      a dark hybrid of fauna and sand. I've seen photographs—
      you share the same eyes. And in mine now, dilating
      these past days, a lighter shade of that carbon glaze and inten-
      tion.

REQUEST ANY IMMINENT MOTHER TO STEP FORWARD (LIT LIKE THE BACKGROUND OF *THE PLOUGH AND THE SONG*, 1947)

And you'll find her
flesh lucent, allowing
something blue to come through

that pulls from a tether to another world, drinks
over curves of hosta. Her skin is the song, dusk brush
strokes. I've felt this

thinning of meat and tissue to house the one
glaze down, the new cache beneath that conceals
itself as it consumes, celebrates its own quiver
and cloaked half covert breadth.

I want to see my unborn infant's face

but can only feel his muted carnival. This canvas—for now
the closest I can get. Something of him in the artist's wash
of painted colostrum. Moss-covered, drift-

wood softened into water-
logged twigs, limbs brittle, but still
he's kicking me. Captured, these small beginnings.

IT IS HUMAN NATURE
TO FILL IN MUTED THINGS
(*GOOD AFTERNOON,*
MRS. LINCOLN, 1944)

And Gorky leaves
only outlines, colours pale as breath.
        Spectral, jade turned ash—

      the man who gave me a silver thimble. There was a time
      I'd memorized all titles on his shelf, seen myself

      in his concessions. Under eyelids, oiled plum. Olbas
      sting, the woman I still love in Vancouver, pinning
      seaweed above her

      light switch, kelp alaria on living room walls. Around us,
ocean
      rasps, hands write on dried magnolia:
                You're never worth your weight
                in salt until you've had a breakdown.

      Broken down. Then, the bringing. Gifts
      of hyssop sticks not long
      out of earth or water. Lust sparks
      northern skin. There is a whole life
      we almost lived together; it shifts

      auroras when skies are clear.
      Solar winds, magnetics. What little we know
      of finishing, of finding
      strength to hold on.

SEVEN YEARS FROM NOW, IN THE UNFINISHED BASEMENT, I'LL FIND MY OLD BOX OF BOOKS ON GORKY

and though some vibrancies need
dark to sleep, it will hurt
to see

how much these years have cost me. By then,
divorce will cut me half-
dead, compressed
in earth's hot mantle. I'll thirst, far away

from my rare magnolia when it rains, the brewed tea
clear in blossoms. I'll search nature:

    a red squirrel and its saliva will empty
      my mouth to glue a new nest for my children. Small Buffleheads
      on the Sydenham, so much time submerged. Needing

            breath, I'll take
            two lovers.

The first will lie about me. Lungs
in THC and ego. Bloodstream, but no keys.
      From Saugeen, an Elder's dried sage will answer.
      Hush, her abalone's ash will say. *Lean away.*

The second man, my last, will speak Spanish
before sleep, free a starling migration. He'll move
murmurations until—for the first time—
I'll start

to let Gorky rest in my mind's
cellar. Trimmed with cyan, we'll leave
our finest pillows for him at the bottom
of the stairs.

PORTRAIT OF MOUGOUCH, PREGNANT, 1943

In the dark hallways of your arms, in the crevices of your chest
are crawlspaces listening to the placenta's red disc, dark
as pitch. A blanket, or is it a coat, opened to orbed breasts
and your belly. My own belly, beginning

to resemble yours. Our babies inside, at this point well-versed
in small stirrings. Did your husband, artist as physician, lift morning
sickness from your skin as he sketched, soothing it
—like balm—with crosshatch? These final days,

my heart is made of acid
and burns. Everything smells of nutmeg, that webbed
seed red with membrane when it splits, a slit
of flesh yielding spice.

SELF-PORTRAITS

I don't take pleasure in looking
at many of his earlier works, the self-
portraits, gaze of the ancients
gone empty. In *Still Life with Horse*, the beast's face
forced down, unable to reach fruit

from the slanted table. Pears and apples
that would taste of glass or sand, cigarette
ash outlining meat and the cracked teeth feeling
of biting tar. Not long ago, that time

pallet knives cut into my life
and I almost gave up having children
for a man, his earth tones too much
like clay to let root another life, in his room a fireplace
that turned on and off

by a switch on the wall. I was never winter
for him, could never probe the physics
of how infinite the vibrating strings, whether we could have
slipped together through a wormhole, into the cavities
of an écorché to rebuild

bones then muscles before lifting over us
a kinder skin.   Strange how it's rare now
for me to ever think of him.

BLUE FIGURE IN A CHAIR, C. 1931

After loss, some women see themselves
in flat colours, cut up into basic shapes. They seek varnish
as gloss, then wrap it around their soundless bodies.

I live with windows ajar under my skin, though there's nothing
to look out onto. Wide-mouthed

voices fog the glass and I'm so
so tired, try to live on the quiet side
of bones. Pull my ribs closed. Scratch darkness
for a clasp. Some think losing

a fetus isn't a real death. Things exist. Then
they don't; I don't

know why I think I should
draw that line. Could someone please dim
the lights? It is too loud
when the seed husks fall without hearts.
On my kitchen island, the entire Arctic

fits in a frosted calla, or is that
a gladiola alone, half bent
by its own kind? Is that my face
in the frame? I've been trying
hard not to ask. The last

of my breast milk makes silk stick
to my skin. Petals beneath petals glued. Soon, this
baby won't drink from me. Crêpe-de-chine.
I'm finding it hard
to feel things.

STILL LIFE WITH SKULL, 1927

Sometimes I sit with the image *Still Life with Skull*, dark cloth
sharpened against bones like my body nested in crushed metal

after colliding on the sea-to-sky highway. The drunken other
unseen; I was afraid a child had died.

The background of the painting a Delphic blue, tilting
at times into white

like my son's umbilical cord before he was cut
from me. He was cut from me, our blood clamped. Last time

I felt pain like that was the car crash. I healed but my words
broke again as they made their way through my body.

Gorky stayed for days with this painting of a skull drowning
with its bones, immersed in muted browns.

I think I've spent time in that same place too,
my Cimmerian manuscript unseen, now housed in another country.

IN SPITE OF MYSELF

Three paintings
of *Image in Khorkom*, and in each
what looks to be a coconut, dead centre, spilling milk—

> the white
> liquid drained
> > from its grated meat,
> > then sweetened. I know
> > these small floods full well

though most literary circles
don't esteem such overflow.

LET HIS CONTOURS AND COLOURS
TAKE YOUR ISLAND

so that they can steal the sand from beneath your feet
and leave you

aqueous. Finned things will make incisions
around your sicknesses, stay still for them

under water. If you become hopeful
and too soon approach a shoal, you'll find
it is a corpse, floating.
                         You must swim, but only swim

where you know they can find you. Stillness
is rigor mortis and you can't safeguard
the heart. Submerged, allow venom, allow
barbs. Allow the stung tips of his
bile, his Devil's Apron swaying
in green blades.

                         *

His unmoored forms are the flight paths
of my fingers as I type the yellow
slur, top centre. I sink and my citrus tongue slides,
knowing lemon preserved in salt
is a much duller colour. Dusk, I should have
spoken the red, its electricity stretched into capillaries
connecting his arteries in this frame to my veins.

                         *

Let go
of the boxed swamp, the crated moss, bloody swell
around the butter knife's entry. The claw beside the maple
plank, wood shavings in umbras, a dove tulip dipped black
by a bleached stingray. Let it unhinge
into graffiti that you can't read—what Woolf's birds said
as she loaded her overcoat with stones.

MAKING THE CALENDAR, 1947

Rising still in the yeast crust the codling moths from apple cores
        the intentions
the regrets the *cri de coeur* left on my laminate counter, small cuts
        where I forgot
how sharp the knife.

PLUMAGE LANDSCAPE, 1947

The placid tongue chassis
encompasses a flesh drip, tinted
like nutmeg melon, as though the word *perhaps*

has spilled within its husk
and curved, then left a stain. Semen, centre milk-
weed, silk seed-nested burr, I stare

where I want to go. I go
where woodchips from trimmed pencils fall and sift
after the slight lift in Gorky's face as he died, his suicide
still the cracked sunlight in an old barn. Last note
scrawled in chalk on a crate: *Goodbye
my Loveds.* Now,

                in the wind, sketching
                on sky, aspen branches tipped with lead and wax,

            a
      whirl

              of maple-
                keys mapp-
                      ing

             his
             part-
                icular

            pigments'
               in-

                flec-
             tions

and rainwater through his body
keeps bringing him
back; I have these moments of his
mud and opal. And root
where the scoured grey sprouts
unvarnished gospel
(not in the centre, a bit
to the left, where the dead bud
is black in its orange blood pod; not above,
where the nubbed lilac rib insists
although it is spring, it is not
green again for everyone.)

CLOSE AT HAND

Arshile, when I drink this city's oak
chlorine, his living imprinted alongside. *Arshile*,
on my tongue the pills he took to sleep
so my body isn't a sieve for the dark answering
machine in the hall. *Arshile*, in my temple's pulse.
In the winter I gave
birth to my son, covered
by a coat trimmed with fox. *Arshile*,
feather-down and white, a languid sweep
of *Arshile* in the rusted smudge
of seeped blood there. Stained blood, I can't
bring myself to bleach it clean. *Arshile*. Cusped
on my teething toddler's gums, a shy surfacing
of eggshell. *Arshile*. In the attic, starless
and indistinct, obsidian. Burnt glistening
of antennae and underwings—when suddenly, this
exposure to light. *Arshile*. Strong throb
of the overripe, November's forgotten
plums, frosted but pristine. *Arshile*.
The slow leak, the knowing
creep of jimson and fleabane in our yard.

DURING THE PANDEMIC, A HIDDEN CANVAS IS DISCOVERED UNDER THE PAPER DARKNESS OF ANOTHER, *UNTITLED (VIRGINIA SUMMER)*, C. 1946–47

Now, this canvas unmuted
in new light.

Laid bare—his scarab, his sea, his stingray's
thrash—not immune. His carotid, his clouds—
no safe distance.

I can take the temperature
of aquamarine or umber, know how
to check paint flecks and an etched
fledgling for fever.

HAVING ASKED

winter aggressive grass and broad hands against the glass the glass pressed across

sun bittercress bearded beggarticks burr marigold under hog plum I have called

skullcap spurge stonecrops to pull for me from Gorky and was answered so that

the low salt strum of his daughters of his embroidery sung undone the solvent

tone of Adoian that sugar-jerked when with too much he touched Mougouch smooth

made of quivering blues and tickseed renewed she was just nineteen clutching caress-

cuddling at his foundling ground-brush breeding what was downed drowned then gold

crowned by who could who could not understand him.

TWO MISCARRIAGES
(*SUMMATION*, 1947)

Under mud, my third baby, before
it could form hard bones. Like the last one
lost, it would rather disintegrate than be scraped
from me, wanting to stay

longer inside but there's no way it can
with no heartbeat. No heart beat. In sleep,

small coins cover skin still fused
over eyelids. Every morning, I wake to day-
lilies that will live their given hours, until.

Mougouch, her obituary
in *The Times*, this
punctuated season
of loss. Her cigarettes
rolled by hand

are ash now, bringing back
these deaths of mine. She said
there is no end to the yes and no
of every aspect of our lives and

they ask
if I want them

cremated, if I want to see what I can feel
unspun in a blood creek. Do I bury them,
perhaps, under a fruit tree
in a green yard, because after all
it is spring now, soon summer. Induced,

all I can do
is spray the naked length
of my body with perfume;
although I can't bring myself
to hold them

I still need them
to sense I am here.
Home, done

with *Summation* I stare
at *The Limit*. Not able
to think

of what this canvas would look like
without

its form, pendulous
on
a

dark
thin cord. No centre

contour that is cello-dulcet
and promising

as a cocoon.
Come loose,

silk

around

pupas.

Clots

become larger the red the red, it hurts
how hollow the unhallowed grey.

The doctor, armed
with a camera that could see
into my womb, called me
sweetheart, said
it was empty.

NOTES

Unless otherwise specified, all references from Hayden Herrera are sourced from her biography *Arshile Gorky: His Life and Work.*

Apprenticeship

According to Herrera, "[i]n the spring of 1915 long lines of Armenians stretched over the countryside as they plodded southward through the dry land toward the Syrian desert" (p. 65). Although I cannot be certain if Gorky's family (the Adoians) encountered Anatolia or the Syrian desert, it is probable since Melissa Kerr of the Arshile Gorky Foundation includes in the foundation's website chronology that "[t]he Adoians join[ed] more than a quarter million refugees on an eight-day, one-hundred-mile journey on foot to Russian Armenia" (Kerr, para. 16 of 281).

Stagnation, Swell, a Sudden Fleshing

The description of hands as "clay blocks" and bricks comes from Matthew Gale, curator of the Tate Modern, in *Arshile Gorky: Enigma and Nostalgia.* About Gorky's 1937 *Self-Portrait*, he notes that the self Gorky portrays has "characteristically amorphous blocked-in hands" (p. 46).

Flame and Smoulder

According to Herrera, Gorky wrote the following to his sister in a letter dated April 18, 1938: "And I have painted my portrait. I have given my eyes the shape of leaves. These two leaves told me constantly YES, yes." (Herrera, p. 299)

Wounded Birds, Poverty, and One Whole Week of Rain

The title for this poem is based on Gorky's response to a 1941 Museum of Modern Art questionnaire. When asked, "Has the subject any special personal, topical or symbolic significance?" Gorky responded, "Wounded birds, poverty and one whole week of rain" (p. 192).

According to Herrera:

[t]he sculptor Reuben Nakian (an American of Armenian origin) told the story:

Gorky and I were in Central Park, sitting on a bench at the lake there. And there were pigeons around, and one of them was hurt and was about to drown. And we were watching as a man from a nearby peanut stand waded in the water to rescue it. So, when it was over, Gorky turned to me and said, "My god, I felt the agony you had." (p. 193)

His Wife, Mougouch, After Her Affair with Matta

Herrera claims that Matta was blamed for Gorky's suicide and labelled a "murderer" by Surrealist leader André Breton (Herrera, p. 623).

The line "How can we, or rather I [unfinished]" was written by Gorky in one of his letters included in Herrera's Gorky biography on pages 615–6.

In Armenia, People Tell Their Bad Dreams to the Running Water

Herrera notes:

Gorky spent a whole Sunday going from butcher shop to butcher shop all over Manhattan, looking for a calf's heart so that he could strip off the heart's surface layer, cure the membrane, and then stretch it over the face of an Armenian stringed instrument that he sometimes strummed to accompany his song. (p. 293)

Cornfield of Health, 1944

According to Herrera, Gorky "called them [apricots] 'those flirts of the sun' and he painted their cleaved and downy lusciousness" (p. 28).

Nighttime, Enigma, and Nostalgia, c. 1931–32

Herrera notes that Gorky's painting *Nighttime, Enigma, and Nostalgia* contains imagery that includes "a bust, a skeletal fish, and a rectangle divided in two by a diagonal. All three are derived from Giorgio de Chirico's *The Fatal Temple* (1913)" (p. 191).

Shards

Herrera states: "When people complained that he [Gorky] was derivative, he would agree: 'Yes, Cezanne is my father, Picasso is my mother.' He insisted that he had the right to learn by imitating his parents" (p. 180).

According to Herrera, Gorky asserted, "I am not drawing the trees. I am drawing the space between the trees" (p. 421).

Herrera notes that "Gorky was named Vosdanig" (p. 22). Vartoosh is the name of Gorky's sister and Shushan is the name of Gorky's mother.

Meditation on White (Traced Backwards)

Herrera notes that the name Shushan means "lily" (p. 30) and that "[m]ost Armenian parents lined the cradle with warm sand covered with cloth" (p. 21). Concerning Shushan, Herrera notes that "every night at bedtime Shushan made sure that her children kneeled facing east and crossed themselves before and after saying the Hail Mary" (p. 31). To preserve food, Herrera notes, when Gorky was a child "[p]ears were hung from the ceiling on strings" (p. 28).

Gorky "did not talk until he was six" (p. 36). Until then, Herrera notes "he spoke only with the birds" (p. 36).

Face to Face with His *Agony*, 1947

In the days after Gorky's serious car accident, Herrera notes that Helena Lam recalled Gorky "standing on the sidewalk, sad and dejected, constantly squeezing a small black rag-type doll in his hand" (Herrera, p. 597).

Upon Stepping Away from *Agony*, 1947

In the book *Bernini's Biographies*, Evonne Levy writes, "in order to study the effect of his own skin and the expression of agony on his own face, which he observed in a mirror, Bernini burned himself" (p. 172).

1940, New York, Gorky Befriends Mondrian

According to V. V. Rankin, who is quoted in Herrera's biography, "Mondrian came [into Gorky's studio] in his English pinstriped suit" (p. 460).

In Herrera's biography, Mougouch recalls that when she saw Gorky in the hospital after his serious car accident, "[h]e was in traction" (p. 592) and "his chin and face [were] drawn back by a 25lb weight" (p. 593).

Herrera states that "[Julien] Levy noticed during his visit [to see Gorky in the hospital] that it was so hot that the white enamel hospital walls were perspiring" (p. 594).

To Project, to Conjure, 1944

In Thierry de Duve's book *Clement Greenberg Between the Lines: Including a Debate with Clement Greenberg*, Greenberg states: "In Pollock, there is [absolutely no] self-deception, and he is not afraid to look ugly—all profoundly original art looks ugly at first...." (Duve, p. 19).

One Thing Shifts into Another, Gorky Dances with Knives

According to Herrera:

> On one occasion Gorky amazed and terrified [...] friends by doing his version of a Russian or Armenian sword dance. He pushed the table aside, picked up two carving knives, and began to sway and sing. As his voice grew louder and his gestures wilder, he leapt in the air, swirling the knives around him and slapping them on his thighs. The artist Charles Mattox recalled: "He was nicking himself. Blood spurted all over the place. He was slipping and dancing in his own blood." (pp. 171–2)

In her poem "After Reading a Poem by Stanley Kunitz," included in the book *Processional*, Anne Compton writes, "Why is back the most beautiful direction?" (p. 28).

From The Moment a Man Is Born, He Looks for a Peaceful Cradle

The title for this poem was inspired by a letter Gorky wrote to his sister Vartush in 1939: "In life, dear Vartush, man has to, since the moment he is born, look for a peaceful cradle" (Herrera, p. 309).

The line "impeccable arrow of light" was inspired by "The Eye Spring," a catalogue written by André Breton for Gorky's first solo show. Breton writes that Gorky's work "can empower a leap beyond the ordinary and the known to indicate, with an impeccable arrow of light, a real feeling of liberty" (Gale, p. 71).

Herrera recounts how "[Gorky and his friends] went to the beach [in Cape Cod] and drew elaborate pictures in the wet sand" (Herrera, p. 248).

Herrera includes the observations of Lewis Balamuth, who remembers how "Gorky rose to his full height in the twilight to emit a loud cry after the manner of the mountain shepherds of his native land" (Herrera, p. 251).

Marny George at 36 Union Square

In Herrera's biography, Marny is quoted as saying, "For six weeks I did not leave the studio" (p. 233). Herrera also recounts a story remembered by Gorky's friend Mischa Reznikoff. She writes:

> Reznikoff ran into the newly betrothed Gorky on Eighth Street coming out of a Russian gift shop with a bundle of little packages wrapped in tissue paper. "Look!" he said as he unwrapped jewelry made of papier-mâché. "Here are my grandmother's jewels!" (p. 231)

Herrera recalls many of Gorky's false identities: "he let it be known he was a Georgian prince" (p. 216). "Reznikoff recalled: 'He always talked of himself as being a Russian rather than an Armenian'" (p. 111). According to a Grand Central School Catalogue discussed by Herrera, Gorky claimed that he studied in Paris at the Académie Julien (p. 131).

Herrera notes: "The night before the wedding [to Marny] Gorky gave a party. Reznikoff and Stuart Davis procured some bootleg liquor and a mass of fruit and vegetables to create an edible still life" (p. 231).

According to Herrera, "Mischa Reznikoff remembered an evening at Ticino's when Marny borrowed Gorky's pen, picked up a bread stick, and wrote on it: 'I would like to be Mrs. Gorky'" (p. 231). Herrera quotes Marny as stating: "It was a moonlight night while crossing the Brooklyn Bridge he asked me to marry him" (p. 231).

Herrera's biography includes quotes by Marny that claim Gorky was violent with her. Herrera recounts Marny's statement:

"First with tenderness, then with force," he tried to "form and mould me into the woman he wanted for his wife." The more violent her husband became, the stronger Marny's resistance grew. (p. 233)

Herrera includes a letter penned by Marny George relating to her early courtship with Gorky. In this letter, Marny remembers receiving from Gorky "a lovely little gardenia tree accompanied [by] a poem" (p. 231) and describes her response to Gorky's artwork as "[a]n act of immediate recognition" (p. 230). She claims he "often stopped to point out the beautiful designs formed by the cracks in the cement sidewalk" (p. 231).

Herrera recounts Mischa Reznikoff's thoughts regarding Marny's appearance: "She looked exactly like that period of Picasso when he had taken off the walls of Pompeii" (p. 232).

See notes for the poem "Face to Face with His Agony, 1947" for quotations relating to rag dolls.

Ambiguous Space, Seemingly Random Angles

Herrera quotes Meyer Shapiro: "Pollock and Rothko and Gottlieb and de Kooning were people who found themselves only after the death of Gorky" (p. 714).

In Duncan Staff's *BBC News* article "Raising the Dead," Professor John Hunter claims that "nettles grow a foot higher over bodies" (Staff, para 26 of 31).

Triptych for Mougouch

The line "a mystery like his aches when it is almost / recognized" is a variation of a statement coined by Richard Capling of Ancaster, Ontario, in a letter to me dated January 10, 2010.

Dear One Absent This Long While

This poem was written in response to Lisa Olstein's poem of the same title included on page 17 of her poetry collection *Radio Crackling, Radio Gone* (Copper Canyon Press).

Studio Fire, 1946

In a January 1946 letter about the studio fire, Mougouch writes: "But as calamities go it had its exhilarating sides—Gorky is a most awesome Phoenix" (Herrera, p. 505).

In a February 1946 letter, Mougouch calls Gorky a "sky miner" (Herrera, p. 507).

The lines *"I am convinced that I cannot exaggerate enough / to even lay the foundation"* are from a 1946 letter Mougouch wrote to Jeanne Reynal in which she attempts to recount the words of Thoreau's *Walden* (Spender, *Goats on the Roof*, p. 305).

It is also inspired by another 1946 letter written by Mougouch to Jeanne Reynal in January 1946 where she states: "Anything that follows is an understatement" (Herrera, p. 504).

During the 1946 studio fire, Herrera notes that "[i]nstead of saving his paintings, he brought out a hammer, a screwdriver, a box of charcoal, and a photograph of his mother and himself at the age of about twelve taken in 1912 in the city of Van" (p. 5).

In the poem "As Kingfishers Catch Fire," Gerard Manley Hopkins writes: "As kingfishers catch fire, dragonflies draw flame."

This Poem Cannot Be Titled

The "feathered onion" is inspired by Gorky's description of an Armenian villager's house. Herrera includes the following description by Gorky:

"In the ceiling was a round aperture to permit the emission of smoke. Over it was placed a wooden cross from which was suspended by a string an onion into which several feathers had been plunged. As each Sunday elapsed, a feather was removed, thus denoting the passage of Time." (p. 20)

André Breton Helps Gorky Title His Work

In what Matthew Spender labels an "unpublished critique of Ethel Schwabacher's biography, c. 1957," Mougouch states:

> Titles, he [Gorky] was told, he must have: the public must have a handle, and so he looked for titles. [...] It was New Year's Eve and he asked M. Breton to help him. Gorky sat and talked of his childhood, talked to each painting as it were, and Breton, with his marvellous incisiveness, made a sign when some particular phrase struck him... (Spender, *Goats on the Roof*, p. 406)

Gorky Finds a Photograph of His Mother, Forgotten in His Father's Drawer

In April 2010, I overheard a staff member at the Tate Modern relay the anecdote of Gorky's father keeping a photograph of his wife Shushan buried in a drawer.

Herrera writes: "According to his grandson George, even after he came to the United States Sedrak always slept with his clothes on and with a hatchet under his pillow" (Herrera, p. 109).

Grief Has No Words, Only a Trailing Off into Things Remembered Inaccurately, *Making the Calendar*, 1947

The title "Grief has no words / only a trailing off into things remembered / inaccurately" is from Anne Simpson's poem "Deer on a Beach" on page two of her book *Light Falls Through You*.

Without Rest

In describing Gorky's capacity for domestic violence, Herrera states that in one instance "Mougouch tried to calm Gorky, but he pushed her away and she stumbled and fell down the stairs. [Mougouch states directly] 'He beat me up and threw me down the stairs'" (p. 600).

Herrera notes that "Gorky was witness to many such beatings, and later in his life, his own physical violence would destroy at least two relationships with women" (p. 43).

Muscles and Tendons, Continued Lines

Herrera states: "Gorky continued to keep 36 Union Square uncluttered and spotless except for his collection of twenty or thirty glass vases. These were allowed to go undusted because he thought dust gave them beautiful colors" (p. 371).

For Maro, Who Was Sent to Boarding School with Her Sister Shortly After

In the *Independent*'s obituary on Mougouch Fielding, it is stated that "Mougouch was remorseful about sending the girls to the Swiss boarding school, saying [...] it was the only thing she 'really regrets'" (para. 12–13 of 15).

In Cosima Spender's (Gorky's granddaughter's) documentary film *Without Gorky* (Peacock Pictures, 2011), Natasha states about her time at the boarding school: "I was spanked every morning for peeing in my bed." Further commenting on her boarding school experience, Maro states: "It was pretty dreadful. I survived better than Natasha. Natasha had a horrible time."

(In the Voice of Natasha) They Have Taken My Island

This poem is a response to Gorky's 1944 painting *They Will Take My Island*. It is also inspired by Cosima Spender's documentary *Without Gorky*, where Natasha is disturbed to the point of tears when observing again the staircase from her childhood home in Sherman, Connecticut, where she last encountered her father alive.

Herrera states:

Maro remembers lying in bed at night listening to her parents fight. One night she woke Natasha up and made her accompany her upstairs to their parents' bedroom. What the girls, five and nearly three, saw was their parents naked and Gorky leaning over their mother as if he were about to hit her. (pp. 598–9)

Things Dissolve in Paint Thinner the Way the Beaten Do with Drink

Herrera writes:

The statement he [Gorky] made about *Garden in Sochi* mentions the liver: "My liver is sick with purple." According to Gorky's nephew Karlen Mooradian, Armenians consider the liver to be the seat of the soul and the center of creative energy. (p. 436)

Tulips, De Kooning's Daughter, and Copper

This poem is based on a photograph of Maro Gorky with Lisa de Kooning on Lee Rosenbaum's blog *CultureGrrl* in her post "Gorgeous Gorky in Philly: Michael Taylor Explains It…All."

After His Death

Herrera notes that "[o]ne exception to the general chorus of praise [for Gorky's work after his death] came from Emily Genauer," who critiqued him unfavourably in the *New York Herald Tribune* on January 7, 1951 (p. 627).

Genauer's review incited the fury of the New York art world. Soon after it appeared she was seated at a dinner party next to a well-known playwright whom she greatly admired. Convinced that Gorky was the greatest American painter of the century, he suddenly turned on her and asked: "Why do you flay dead dogs?" (p. 627)

The third stanza of this poem is based on information gleaned from Herrera's biography. Relaying an incident in a museum while Gorky was examining work with his students, Herrera notes: "[T]hey continued to look at Coptic embroideries. 'Better than Matisse,' Gorky pronounced" (p.149). Herrera notes that Gorky, as a child, would have encountered in a garden close to his home "a long-dead pine called a *pshad* tree, which spread out along the ground for about thirty meters. Considered holy, it was called the tree of the cross or the tree of wish fulfilment" (p. 31). Regarding the women from Gorky's childhood community, Herrera notes that "[t]o prepare [for Easter], they boiled eggs in water with onion-skins so that the eggs turned deep reddish brown" (p. 51). Describing Gorky's physical appearance, Herrera notes: "His orphan eyes were irresistible" (p. 228). Herrera repeats the following quote from Gorky pertaining to his painting *The Liver Is the Cock's Comb*: "The song of a cardinal, liver, mirrors that have not caught reflection" (p. 436).

Plumage Landscape, 1947

Hayden Herrera, in an article written for *Vogue* entitled "Arshile and Agnes Gorky: Master and Muse," describes details of Gorky's suicide: "Having left ropes dangling from various trees and rafters, Gorky hanged himself in a shed. He left a note written in chalk on the box he stood on and kicked away: 'Goodbye my loveds'" (Herrera, *Vogue*, para. 18 of 21).

During the Pandemic, a Hidden Canvas Is Discovered Under the Paper Darkness of Another, *Untitled (Virginia Summer)*, c. 1946–47

In *Smithsonian Magazine*, Nora McGreevy's article "This Arshile Gorky Painting Spent 70 Years Hidden in Plain Sight" states that during a Covid-19 lockdown, "[c]onservators discovered this painting, *Untitled (Virginia Summer)*, beneath another work by Gorky, *The Limit* (1947)."

Two Miscarriages (Summation, 1947)

Herrera notes that in a letter to Ethel Schwabacher, Mougouch writes: "There is no end to the yes and no of every aspect of our life" (Herrera, p. 622).

BIBLIOGRAPHY

Berry, Nicole, "Arshile Gorky: A Retrospective at the Philadelphia Museum of Art," *Accessible Art*, 2009 <accessibleartny.com/index. php/2009/11/arshile-gorky-a-retrospective-at-the-philadelphia-museum-of-art/>

Breton, André, "The Eye-Spring, Arshile Gorky," *Arshile Gorky* (Julien Levy Gallery: New York, 1945), quoted in Matthew Gale, *Arshile Gorky: Enigma and Nostalgia* (London: Tate Publishing, 2010)

Capling, Richard, personal letter to author (Ancaster, Ontario, 10 January 2010)

Carson, Anne, "Book of Isaiah," in *Glass, Irony, and God* (New York: New Directions, 1995)

Compton, Anne, "After Reading a Poem by Stanley Kunitz," in *Processional* (Markham: Fitzhenry & Whiteside, 2005)

Gale, Matthew, *Arshile Gorky: Enigma and Nostalgia* (London: Tate Publishing, 2010)

Giraudon, Collette, "Chaim Soutine (French, 1893–1943)," *MoMA: The Collection*, 2009 <www.moma.org/collection/artist.php?artist_id=5543>

Greenberg, Clement, "Art," *The Nation*, 7 April 1945, quoted in Thierry de Duve, *Clement Greenberg Between the Lines: Including a Debate with Clement Greenberg*, trans. Brian Holmes (Chicago: University of Chicago Press, 2010)

Herrera, Hayden, "Arshile and Agnes Gorky: Master and Muse," *Vogue*, December 2009 <www.vogue.com/magazine/article/arshile-and-agnes-gorky-master-and-muse/#1>

——— *Arshile Gorky: His Life and Work* (New York: Farrar, Straus and Giroux, 2003)

Hughes, Ted, *Letters of Ted Hughes*, ed. Christopher Reid (London: Faber and Faber, 2011)

Kerr, Melissa, "Chronology," The Arshile Gorky Foundation <arshilegorkyfoundation.org/gorkys-life>

Kirkup, James, trans., "Sonnet, Stephane Mallarme," 2001 <www. brindin.com/pfmalson.htm>

Levy, Evonne, "Chapter 2 of Domenico Bernini's Vita of His Father: Mimeses," in *Bernini's Biographies*, ed. Maarten Delbeke, Evonne Levy, and Steven F. Ostrow (Pennsylvania: Penn State Press, 2006)

Levy, Paul, "Mougouch Fielding: Painter Who Became Muse to Arshile Gorky," *The Independent*, 2013 <www.independent.co.uk/news/obituaries/mougouch-fielding-painter-who-became-muse-to-arshile-gorky-8745437.html>

McGreevy, Nora. "This Arshile Gorky Painting Spent 70 Years Hidden in Plain Sight," *Smithsonian Magazine*, 2021 <https://www.smithsonianmag.com/smart-news/arshile-gorky-painting-discovery-hidden-180978950/>

"Impressions of London's Tate Modern," *London Liaison: Londoner for a Year*, 2012 <londonliaison.wordpress.com/2012/04/20/some-impressions-of-londons-tate-modern/>

"Rembrandt: 1606–1669," The National Gallery <www.nationalgallery.org.uk/artists/rembrandt>

Olstein, Lisa, "Dear One Absent This Long While," in *Radio Crackling, Radio Gone* (Port Townsend: Copper Canyon Press, 2006)

Without Gorky, dir. Cosima Spender (Peacock Pictures, 2011)

"Rainer Maria Rilke," Poetry Foundation <www.poetryfoundation.org/bio/rainer-maria-rilke>

Rand, Harry, *Arshile Gorky: The Implications of Symbols* (Berkeley: University of California Press, 1991)

Rosenbaum, Lee, "Gorgeous Gorky in Philly: Michael Taylor Explains It All," *CultureGrrl: Lee Rosenbaum's Cultural Commentary*, 2009 <www.artsjournal.com/culturegrrl/2009/10/gorgeous_gorky_in_philly_micha.html>

Simpson, Anne, *Light Falls Through You* (Toronto: McClelland & Stewart, 2000)

Spender, Matthew, ed., *Arshile Gorky, Goats on the Roof: A Life in Letters and Documents* (London: Ridinghouse, 2009)

Staff, Duncan, "Raising the Dead," *BBC News*, 2005 <news.bbc.co.uk/1/hi/magazine/4415346.stm>

ACKNOWLEDGEMENTS

Thank you to Denis De Klerck, publisher of Mansfield Press, for believing in this work, and the Ontario Arts Council for their generosity.

I would like to express my deepest gratitude to Dr. Katherine Stansfield, who made this book possible. Thank you, Stuart Ross, for holding a flashlight as I found my way back.

Thank you to my poetry kindreds, Christine McNair and Richard Capling. I am grateful to Marnie Buffett, Janice Colbert, Stacey Tiller, rob mclennan, Faye Fisher, Ken Horrell, Ilke Humphries, Val Davies, and Jen Boucher for the beauty of who they are. With my heart, I would like to remember Charles Fisher, who recently passed at the age of 107; he will be in every monarch butterfly my children and I see. Thank you to Anne Simpson, who helped me keep the faith. Thank you to Cosima Spender; her profound documentary *Without Gorky* deepened my understanding. Thank you to early poetry mentors Marilyn Gear Pilling and Margaret Christakos, as well as Diaspora Dialogues. I am appreciative of the Bedfordshire National Open Poetry Awards, as well as Dr. Kelly Grovier and the Creative Writing Department at Aberystwyth University. A heartfelt thank-you to Rhea Tregebov and the UBC Creative Writing Program for helping me build a foundation.

I would like to express gratitude for my grandfather, Eric Dennis, who first paved my writing way. Alongside the memory of Elizabeth Smith, my grandmother, I'd like to place coral rose petals. I am appreciative of my father, William Dennis—a source of laughter and support—and the kind generosity of my stepmother, Helen Dennis. Thank you to my grandmother Margaret Dennis, for her elegance and love. Thank you to Mark Nimigan, who always believed in me and was the first to offer champagne. Thank you to Andrew Cook for the meals cooked, tea brewed, friendship grown, and for being a wonderful father to our two children.

I cannot express the depth of appreciation I have for my mother, Victoria Dennis. At every turn, she reaches with luminosity, adding another layer of nacre.

Thank you to Alberto Bassi, amor de mi vida, for the love letters he hides around our house. His strength, passion, tenderness, and wingspan make me a better person.

Most importantly, thank you to my two sons, Finnian and Rilke, who resonate with all things beautiful. May Finn never stop playing "BlackBird" on his guitar, and may Rilke continue to celebrate life with joie de vivre; it is no wonder the first word he learned to spell was *joy*.

ABOUT THE AUTHOR

Amy Dennis received her MFA through the University of British Columbia and studied creative writing at Harvard University's Extension School. In addition to publications in England and France, Amy's poetry has appeared in more than twenty Canadian literary publications, including *CV2, Event, Queen's Quarterly,* and *Prairie Fire.* Her poetry has been nominated for two National Magazine Awards and a Random House Creative Writing Award. She placed second in the UK's National Bedford Open Poetry Competition. Her chapbook *The Complement and Antagonist of Black (Or, The Definition of All Visible Wavelengths)* was published by above/ground press. She completed her PhD with distinction in ekphrastic poetry and new confessionalism. She works as a professor and learning facilitator.